WISE AS A SERPENT
INNOCENT AS A DOVE

WISE AS A SERPENT
INNOCENT AS A DOVE

Alexys V. Wolf

Wise as a Serpent, Innocent as a Dove

Scripture quotations marked "NAS" are taken from the New American Standard Bible ®, Copyright © 1960, 1962, 1963, 1968, 1971, 1972, 1973, 1975, 1977, 1995 by The Lockman Foundation. Used by permission. All rights reserved.

Cover design by Alexys Vaulkenroth of *The Camel's Brush*

Cover photo by Alexys Vaulkenroth of *The Camel's Brush*

Interior design by CreateSpace Independent Publishing Platform, North Charleston, South Carolina

The opinions expressed by the author are those of The Fiery Sword Ministries.

CreateSpace Independent Publishing Platform

North Charleston, South Carolina

Published in the United States of America

ISBN-13: 978-1542623698

ISBN-10: 1542623693

1. Religion / Christian Life / Personal Growth

2. Religion / Christian Life / Spiritual Growth

TABLE OF CONTENTS

TABLE OF CONTENTS

AUTHOR BIO

Alexys V. Wolf is the founder of the non-profit organization, *The Fiery Sword Ministries*, and is in love with our most Holy God. She earnestly desires to assist people from every walk of life to come out of the darkness of religiosity and into the light of the Kingdom of God. Her vision is to guide people out of carnally-driven Christianity into a Spirit-led, Spirit-driven, Kingdom-minded life full of joy. This allows God's people to usher Heaven down to Earth as is God's original intent.

Alexys began her ministry preaching and teaching in prisons and has since been a guest on TV, radio, and conferences as well as ministering to people globally via internet and phone. Her mission statement is that of Jesus' found in Luke 4:18-19: "*to preach the gospel to the poor, to proclaim release to the captives, and recovery of sight to the blind, to set free those who are oppressed, and to proclaim the favorable year of the Lord.*" She has several published books and, if you're interested in inviting her as a guest speaker, please contact her at thefierysword@windstream.net or 803-238-5166. For more information, her website address is www.thefierysword.com.

INTRODUCTION

"Behold, I send you forth as sheep in the midst of wolves. Be ye therefore wise as serpents and harmless as doves (Matthew 10:16, KJV)."

We don't hear much about wisdom in the modern-day churches and, when we do, we hear little about innocence. This day and age is a time of self-serving religion on its best day, not to mention what it is on the worst of days! The King James Version reads "*harmless* as a dove" whereas the New American Standard reads, "… *innocent* as doves." Either way, I see a lot of wise people who can preach, teach, prophesy, and more, yet they lack the ability to be innocent or harmless, aka gentle.

This book is designed to bring the body of Christ, especially leaders of any vocation, to learn what it is to be innocent and wise at the same time. There's a very good reason as to why God gave such explicit instruction; it's because He understands that, like Lucifer, we can be the wisest of them all yet allow our wisdom to be corrupted by pride.

CHAPTER 1

WHAT IS WISDOM

"Who among you is wise and understanding? Let him show by his good behavior his deeds in the gentleness of wisdom…but the wisdom from above is first pure, then peaceable, gentle, reasonable, full of mercy and good fruits, unwavering, without hypocrisy (James 3:13, 17, NAS)."

The world most assuredly has its own version of wisdom. It apparently has everything to do with how to make the most money, how to get what makes one feel better about self, and so on. Wisdom of the Earth revolves around self-gratification. Contrarily, heavenly wisdom has everything to do with holiness, that which is pleasing to Yahweh. Its characteristics are purity, peace, gentleness, reasonable, merciful, bearing good fruits, immovable and impartiality.

This is without question nothing like that of the world. There are times when worldly wisdom can in fact sound the same on the surface, but even so, the motivation behind the words are vastly differing. It is imperative for the body of Christ to be able to discern the difference between that of the world and that of Heaven lest we continuously be led astray by the tactics of the enemy of God. The only way to obtain such discernment is, as you know, to be led by the Spirit of God instead of any other source.

If you personally are questioning whether or not you are operating in the King's wisdom, ask yourself, "Is my point of view pure? Peaceable? Gentle? Reasonable? Merciful? Going to bear good fruits? Unwavering? Impartial? If the answer is "no" to any of these, you need to reevaluate your perspective prior to delving advice.

NOTES

_____

_____

_____

_____

_____

_____

_____

_____

_____

_____

_____

_____

_____

_____

THE LORD GIVES WISDOM

"For the LORD GIVES WISDOM; from His mouth come knowledge and understanding (Proverbs 2:6, NAS)."

I hear people all the time speak in a manner lacking in wisdom. They spew nonsense which feels good to them and with words that are clearly not thoroughly processed. Advice, for lack of a better term, is strewn about never thinking about the consequences those words will have for the recipient. We don't operate in wisdom because, frankly, we have not sought the face of God so as to receive such heavenly wisdom. Since He has previously promised to give wisdom for those who ask, we can deduce wisdom is absent because we haven't endeavored to gain wisdom from the Wisdom giver.

In this age, people have become (as biblically prophesied) lovers of self; lovers of pleasures more than lovers of God (II Timothy 3). The love of self is the opposite of loving God, His Word, His wisdom and understanding. Yes, we should love ourselves so as to be able to love others as we love ourselves, but that is more of a 'respecting ourselves' type love. Contrarily, that of which the Bible speaks is a self-serving, self-appeasing love. When we're loving ourselves in this manner, we've become an idol unto ourselves set above and against God.

Unfortunately, the biblical reference is not referring to the world, for they never loved God. It is a description of the Church, those who are supposed to love, honor, reverence, and cherish the Lord Jesus Christ. At the root, we lost sight because we lost our fear of the Lord.

Beginning of Wisdom and Understanding:

"The fear of the Lord is the beginning of wisdom, and the knowledge of the Holy One is understanding (Proverbs 9:10, NAS)."

"The fear of the Lord is the beginning of wisdom; a good understanding have all those who do His commandments; His praise endures forever (Psalm 111:10, NAS)."

So many modern-day Christians do a lot of biblical stuff but they haven't actually come to a place where they whole-heartedly fear the Lord. I know firsthand because I was one of them. I loved the Lord as much as I knew how, but it wasn't until God brought me flat down on my face on the ground that I began to experience the fear of the Lord. Church attendance, saying with emotion a prayer of salvation, doing good deeds, etc. are not necessarily coming from a place of the fear of the Lord but merely a place of good intentions. Fear of the Lord is not what drives most Christians, as sad of a fact as that is.

God's people are a peculiar people, a holy nation. Because of this, wisdom and understanding of His Word are not optional. The only way to operate in true holiness is to obtain and maintain wisdom combined with understanding which begins with fearing the Almighty.

NOTES

CALLED TO WISDOM

"But if any of you lacks wisdom, let him ask of God, who gives to all generously and without reproach, and it will be given to him (James 1:5, NAS)."

Some view this Scripture as, "Hey, if I want wisdom, I can ask God and He'll grant it. I'll just let Him know if and when I decide I need it" but this attitude couldn't be further from righteousness. As stated at the close of the last chapter, wisdom and understanding are not an option for anyone who longs to walk in the purity of holiness and the life Jesus walked.

What this passage is actually doing is making the point that no one possesses a valid excuse for walking in foolishness, no one. God is a generous God and He is faithful to His word and His promises therein. God does not withhold good from His people, from those who seek His purpose. He would not send ambassadors from Heaven into the Earth ill-prepared. No one who has walked with Christ any length of time can rightly exclaim, "I didn't know better. I wasn't wise enough to make such a monumental decision," whatever that decision may be.

For every person of any age, gender, race, nationality, social status, political view, or geographical address, wisdom is readily available. All one must do is humble him or herself so as to position themselves to ask and receive. There is nothing in God's Kingdom He has not granted His people through His Spirit. I often chuckle to myself when people ask me, "Alexys, pray that I have wisdom in this or that." I'm not making fun of them, rather it's a sad chuckle that most people who claim to follow Christ do not yet understand that Christ *is* wisdom; therefore, if Christ be in them, wisdom in its fullness also resides.

The same can be said for gentleness, kindness, patience, love, joy, peace, goodness, self-control, mercy, grace, and so much more. So really, at the root, asking for wisdom is more a matter of asking for Jesus to become our life source so that, whenever we need that which is from Heaven, the supply was made prior to our request. Asking requires humility. In humility, we are poised to receive that which we could not attain when we were too pridefully embarrassed to ask for anything. Humility is vital when asking Christ to become our heart. Everything about the Kingdom of God, anything we could possibly ever need or want that is of any eternal value can come only through humbling ourselves.

In this understanding, we can read James 1:5 with a new perspective. One that reveals we are all called to wisdom and the only way to obtain it is to humble ourselves and ask. The asking isn't because God wants to embarrass us, but because He wants us humble so that we will have access to all that is His in His Kingdom. This is why most "Christians" are potentially saved from hell, but not at all from the elements of this condemned Earth. There's no humility, hence no wisdom attached to our knowledge because there's no fear of God. When there's no fear (reverence) of God, we miss all the benefits, all the armor of God, all the attributes of God. No fear of God = no humility = no wisdom.

People of God, we are called to wisdom because without it, we will fail in our walk with Christ. We must humble ourselves, ask, receive, and go and walk in all the privileges of the Lord. Be confident that, if we are hidden in Christ, we have all that is in Him.

NOTES

CHAPTER 4

BETTER THAN SILVER AND GOLD

"How much better it is to get wisdom than gold! And to get understanding is to be chosen above silver (Proverbs 16:16, NAS)."

"It is easier for a camel to go through the eye of the needle than for a rich man to enter into the Kingdom of God (Mark 10:25, NAS)."

Wisdom from above is priceless, no two ways about it. This world strives endlessly to achieve reputation, status and wealth, to attain worldly possessions only to find themselves possessed by their possessions. Who needs a demon to possess them when they have riches, reputation, fame and fortune to possess them all the more? I'm wondering when God's people will begin to appreciate the value of wisdom. Proverbs 16:16 states without pause, wisdom is better than gold and understanding better than silver. What a proclamation!

I know so many people who say they value wisdom, yet they don't seek understanding of that same wisdom; one without the other makes void the one you do have. Some folks have understanding but have not wisdom to put that understanding to good use. For instance, I may have the wisdom to do the commands of God, but if I do not understand why I'm doing them, I may easily fall away because they become as nonsense. We who are of a peculiar nation need both wisdom and understanding so as to not only survive this life, but to be thriving and successful in our Kingdom endeavors.

It's time we start devaluing the things of this Earth, both tangible and intangible, and begin to shift our affections toward that which God calls better than all those things. It stems back to the scenario of the camel going through the eye of a needle. A rich man places his value and security in his monetary wealth. What he fears is not God, but losing his riches. His fear is displaced and, in this, he cannot possibly reverently fear the Lord God. There is no wisdom in this mindset. If the rich man cannot obtain wisdom from above, he will die missing the Kingdom of God.

Only when we shift our focus onto the King of kings will we be equipped spiritually, mentally and emotionally to enter the eternal Kingdom of God and to operate in His wisdom while residing on Earth. Silver and gold will pass away but God's Kingdom is forever and ever. Zephaniah 1:18 states this: "Neither silver nor their gold will be able to deliver them on the day of the Lord's wrath; and all the Earth will be devoured in the fire of His jealousy, for He will make a complete end, indeed a terrifying one, of all the inhabitants of the Earth."

NOTES

_____

_____

_____

_____

_____

_____

_____

_____

_____

_____

_____

_____

_____

_____

CHAPTER 5

SEASONED WITH SALT AND FULL OF GRACE

"Therefore be careful how you walk, not as unwise men but as wise, making the most of your time, because the days are evil (Ephesians 5:15-16, NAS)."

"Conduct yourselves with wisdom toward outsiders, making the most of the opportunity. Let your speech always be with grace, as though seasoned with salt, so that you will know how you should respond to each person (Colossians 4:5-6, NAS)."

Here we can affirm our previous stance on being called to wisdom. It is the foolish of this world, and primarily those of the body of Christ, who do not make the most of their time on Earth as it is brief. So many running about their daily lives busy with this or that, attending church services regularly, fussing and worrying over their families, friends, co-workers, and enemies, yet in all this, they are so preoccupied with the earthly, they miss their Kingdom calling. In this alone, we are unwise. Worry is of Satan, not God, so it is foolish. Busyness instead of taking time for rest and solitude is equally foolhardy. Replacing God with church activities and services is not of God.

There's so much we do in this life that is beyond worthless yet we see ourselves as Christ-like. This is not wisdom. We are not redeeming the time God has granted. The days are most assuredly evil. The days are more and more about man, man's desires, man's lusts of the flesh, and what pleases him or her. Especially within the confines of the church, there is idiocy running rampant. All the anger, resentment, division, malice, perversion, adultery, fornication, excusing sin, calling what is good evil, calling what is evil good, lethargy, and more are going on right in our midst among those who call themselves "of Christ".

If I may add, a "Christian" is not necessarily the same as a "follower of Christ"; the variance is large as the term "Christian" is vague. A mainstream Christian can be anywhere from someone who loves God to someone who simply believes He exists without living a Christ-filled life. A "follower of Christ", adversely, is someone who is utterly surrendered to the King of kings and devoted to Kingdom work. I've noticed in the last several years, the church has adopted the term "follower of Christ" and everyone is using it. It's like how the term "Kingdom" has become popular so mainstream Christians are saying "Kingdom" when they haven't a clue what being Kingdom-minded even means. It sounds good, so they adopt the terms as their own. This is imprudence. Wisdom will dictate we become less busy and more intimate with Christ and, in such intimacy, we'll willingly humble ourselves, seek wisdom and understanding and go and be as Christ has called, not what some person said might be a good idea.

I have prayed Colossians 4:5-6 over myself many, many years; that my words be seasoned with salt and full of grace. I pray this because I know that, in my fleshly nature, I can be too salty and lacking grace. We are called to conduct ourselves in wisdom. Both Ephesians and Colossians note that we are to make the most of time and opportunity. This is because we may never have another opportunity to be the light of the Kingdom in that particular situation or with that person or group of people.

Furthermore, we are to conduct ourselves with wisdom with outsiders. I love this for the correction it brings me personally. How many times have I been rude not considering I'll ever see that person again so I have acted as though it doesn't matter how I handle them. It is vital we use wisdom when dealing with those close to us and those who are strangers. We never know what impact we will make on them either for good or bad.

This is why we must be wise always, not just when we think we need wisdom. Wisdom is for every moment of every day. Understanding this valuable instruction can actually change someone's life for the Kingdom though we may never know this side of Heaven.

Watch your words and actions. Be wise. Be kind. Be as Christ.

NOTES

CHAPTER 6

THE KEY TO LOVING LIFE

"He who gets wisdom loves his own soul; he who keeps understanding will find good (Proverbs 19:8, NAS)."

Wow, what a statement of power and peace! Here we are again with both wisdom and understanding in the same text; they go hand in hand. I want to look at the first part of this text. "He who gets wisdom loves his own soul" is an empowering statement. The opposite of this would be, "He who doesn't get wisdom, hates his soul." Hmmmm…that's something to ponder, at least for me.

It stands to reason that, if one loves his or her own soul, he or she will love this life because, in their wisdom, it will be accompanied by joy. They will have obtained wisdom through God which will lead them to seek understanding which will lead to boundless possibilities. When I operate in *wisdom* and its sister, *understanding*, everything is much less difficult, must less stressful. This is because wisdom from Heaven is nothing like that of Earth. People operating in their fleshly wisdom base everything on the pride of life. They pride themselves on how smart, wise, and talented they are in being capable of defusing a bad situation or solving a problem. Alongside that pride comes the stress and the pressure of never making a mistake and always having to be better than or as smart as the last time they accomplished something good. This causes stress, anxiety and unrest.

On the other hand, functioning in the wisdom from Heaven comes through humility, as previously discussed. In such wisdom and humility, one is aware that nothing good they accomplish is of them. In turn, there is no stress, no pressure, no anxiety of hoping they'll do it right the next time and no need of attempting to be better than the last wise decision. Wise people simply flow with Holy Spirit each and every time they are faced with a challenge; all the pressure is on God who can handle it. When there is no stress, one is free to love life. When one loves their own soul, they are free to love others without stipulations, coercion, control or manipulation. One thing connects to the other.

A person who loves their own soul is one who seeks wisdom. Wisdom is resting in Christ. Wisdom is peace in the midst of a trial. Wisdom is knowing that, though they may not see results immediately, God has already resolved their issue, no matter how big or small. Wisdom allows one to be kind to strangers, to make the most of time, opportunities and situations and allows them to see as Christ, not merely as what's right in front of them. Wisdom from Heaven grants a God-perspective. Understanding, then, comes along and glues it all together. Recognizing wisdom and understanding are more precious than anything of this Earth will free us to love this life with all its twists and turns, trials and tribulations.

NOTES

WISDOM REQUIRES FOOLISHNESS

"Let no man deceive himself. If any man among you thinks that he is wise in this age, he must become foolish, so that he may become wise (I Corinthians 3:18, NAS)."

Indeed, I count everything as loss because of the surpassing worth of knowing Christ Jesus my Lord. For His sake I have suffered the loss of all things and count them as rubbish, in order that I may gain Christ and be found in Him, not having a righteousness of my own that comes from the law, but that which comes through faith in Christ, the righteousness from God that depends on faith – that I may know Him and the power of His resurrection, and may share His sufferings, becoming like Him in His death.

Philippians 3:8-10 (ESV)

"For by the grace of God given to me I say to everyone of you not to think more highly of himself and of his importance and ability than he ought to think; but to think so as to have sound judgment, as God has apportioned to each a degree of faith and a purpose designed for service (Romans 12:3, AMP)."

Aaaaaahhhhh, I love this! It's so confounding to the non-believer and even the "Christian" who hasn't become a true follower of Christ. No one, and I mean no one, says of his own fleshly minded volition, "I want to become foolish!" When people are operating under the power of their old man, they strive and struggle to become wise in the eyes of man. They want to look brilliant, wise, smart, shrewd, or whatever appeases their ego. When they think they've attained these things, they boast to themselves or to others about their own achievements. Pride comes before the fall which is why we see countless people rise to fame and fortune yet eventually crash to the proverbial ground and burn as nothing.

We've witnessed this with high profile ministers, politicians, corporate moguls, billionaires, celebrities and more. It's because they were wise in their own eyes. This person or group of people did not make themselves as a fool. This does not mean someone becomes the village idiot but rather it does mean they humble themselves to the point of surrendering self unto our holy God. It's a place of taking up their cross (death) recognizing that, no matter how great they think themselves or others think they are, they count it all as loss. The word "all" we read in Philippians 3 above encompasses not only material wealth, but reputation before God and man. The latter is a far more valuable item than the former. True heavenly wisdom will dictate we place no value on anything of this world.

When a person is in the minority rejecting the goods, fame and fortune of this Earth, they most definitely look as a fool to onlookers. Becoming a "fool" is relinquishing anything of self over to the One who created Heaven and Earth. It's the concept, "there's no one good but God" which were the words of Jesus who was God in the flesh. Christ must have appeared as a fool to Satan and his demons by deferring to God. Jesus took no pride in being the Great I AM. Humility, humility, humility. It always appears as foolishness to the prideful, those who think more highly of themselves than they ought.

Denying self, a requirement of receiving Christ and His Kingdom, is foolish to the fleshly, but it's in our denial of self where we can ever hope to operate in the wisdom from God.

NOTES

WHAT S THE BIG DEAL ABOUT THE

SERPENT

"Now the serpent was more crafty than any beast of the field which the Lord God had made...(Genesis 3:1, NAS)."

The Lord sent fiery serpents among the people and they bit the people, so that many people of Israel died. So the people came to Moses and said, "We have sinned, because we have spoken against the Lord and you; intercede with the Lord, that He may remove the serpents from us." And Moses interceded for the people. Then the Lord said to Moses, "Make a fiery serpent, and set it on a standard; and it shall come about, that everyone who is bitten, when he looks at it, he will live." And Moses made a bronze serpent and set it on the standard; and it came about, that if a serpent bit any man, when he looked to the bronze serpent, he lived.

Numbers 21:6-9 (NAS)

"As Moses lifted up the serpent in the wilderness, even so must the Son of Man be lifted up (John 3:14, NAS)."

First, we're all familiar with the words of Genesis 3:1 where we see notated the "serpent was more crafty than any beast of the field". From the beginning, God makes certain we understand how sly the serpent is and we all know that, for anyone to be crafty successfully, one must be wise so as to know how to operate in such an artistically manipulative way. Many people are crafty but their ignorance keeps them from proper delivery. Lucifer had to operate in wisdom well enough to know what and how to speak to Eve so as to deceive her successfully.

Secondly, we read in Numbers 21 and John 3 that Jesus is compared to a serpent...wait, what?! How can this be? Why would God compare Jesus with a serpent? Simple: because there had to be a cure for death. The serpent caused the death curse and Christ cured it. Pre-resurrection, making and lifting a bronze image of a serpent and instructing the sinful Israelites to look upon it so as to cure the fiery serpents' bites was a symbol of things to come. Their sin, grumbling against

God in the wilderness, was caused by the ultimate serpent, Lucifer.

Just as Eve gave way to the cunningness of Lucifer, so did the Israelites. Just as a curse came upon Eve, Adam, and all mankind, likewise, the curse of the fiery snakes came to the Israelites. Looking to a lifted brass graven image of a serpent (otherwise a sin against God) for the cure to their death was an act causing the people to humble themselves by looking upon their own sin and its creator. They had to look at the cause from which they otherwise were to look away. They chose sin; therefore, they had to face their sin. I read on Bible.org, "Jesus is saying that the Spirit of God cannot just brush away sin when He grants the new birth. For sin to be dealt with, God's justice must be satisfied. The Son of Man must be lifted up to satisfy God's wrath on behalf of sinners who believe in Him."

Jesus was lifted up in due season and He was the cure for our sin. He bore the sin of all mankind and we must, current day, look at Christ for the cure. Both the Israelites pre-resurrection as well as we today post-resurrection had to look upon our sin as an act of utter humility. God's wrath must be justified by confronting the sin of man. Jesus bore our sins and, in so doing, when we look at Christ, we look at our sin in order to be redeemed by the one who carried our sin.

The serpent was "lifted up" which is a show of pride – the cause of their fall. Christ was "lifted up" in order to humble us from the fall of pride which resulted in His death. The serpent was a symbol of sin and judgment. Christ was a symbol of righteousness and redemption through bearing the sin and judgment of man. Furthermore, it was an act of faith for healing.

In context, it is imperative to understand the power of the symbol of the serpent. Lucifer was the wisest of all God's creation, barring only Himself. Satan had enough wisdom to rule on the high mountain of God and the Garden of Eden (pre-Adam and Eve), so there's something to learn for sure. Take a look at the level of Lucifer's wisdom depicted in Ezekiel 28:

Behold, you are wiser than Daniel; there is no secret that is a match for you. By your wisdom and understanding you have acquired riches for yourself and have acquired gold and silver for your treasuries. By your great wisdom, by your trade you have increased your riches and your heart is lifted up because of your riches...you were in Eden, the garden of God...you were the anointed cherub who covers, and I placed you there. You were on the holy mountain of God.

Ezekiel 28:3-5, 13-14 (NAS)

Though, as we well know, his wisdom became tainted by pride. God wants us to be as wise as a serpent, yet innocent as a dove so as not to go the way of prideful Cain, aka Lucifer who tempted Cain. Lucifer was wiser than all, yet bore no innocence which would have kept him pure. Many shallow Christians and even some genuine Christ-followers are innocent, yet bear no wisdom to keep them from harm. In that condition, they are truly lambs at the slaughtering house.

God purposefully and strategically instructs His people to be wise as a serpent and innocent as doves because both are a requirement for a successful journey on this Earth. Much like wisdom and understanding must merge as one, so must innocence and wisdom.

NOTES

CHAPTER 9

WHEN PRIDE COMES

"When pride comes, then comes dishonor, but with the humble is wisdom (Proverbs 11:2, NAS)."

I just read in the news yesterday that some famous pastor in Florida was literally caught with his pants down while having sex with a married member of his congregation. The woman's husband walked in on them while in the act of adultery. Why, one may ask, would someone who is such a pillar of the community and church who preaches so wisely be so stupid? In my estimation, it has to be he didn't understand the wisdom God granted which was to coincide knowledge of the Word.

With the absence of understanding the *why* of God's instruction, pride moves into its empty space. For instance, God calls His people to holiness and to abstain from sexual sin. The *why* of this command is, as it is with every command, God's faithful protection over

His people. If a person of God knows the instruction intellectually but is lacking personal understanding that it's from God's heart of love, one will easily stray when temptation presents itself. Pride will call the wisest of men and women to fall with exceeding disgrace.

Then, as I read further, the article stated this pastor stood before his congregation "repentant" and asked for grace and mercy. The response of the congregation was they stood and applauded this man with the plan to keep him in his pastoral position. I ask you, where is the wisdom? I'm all about grace and mercy, but there must be correction especially for God's leaders. James 3:1 plainly states, "Let not many of them become teachers, my brethren, knowing that as such we will incur a stricter judgment." There must be true repentance prior to one being reestablished in their Kingdom role lest they lead astray multitudes.

As a side note, the congregants probably thought they were being forgiving as we are called to be, but this is misguided. Forgiveness is one thing, but allowing him to remain in a position of leadership is errant based on James 3:1. What the people failed to recognize is that wayward people need time to step back, repent, and restructure their relationship with Christ so that obedience to the Lord will rule. One cannot rightly preach to others while being blatantly disobedient. Whether or not he was sincere in his "repentance" is between him and God. Nevertheless, he still should remove himself so as to get his life back on spiritual track.

In this scenario, the pastor only deigned to repent because he was caught, not because he was truly remorseful. He admitted his sins to the church, not of his own volition, but because it was the only option to maintain his position in the church given he was caught with his pants down. I see this all the time in ministries. Someone gets caught, they give some feeble words of repentance and then move on as if nothing happened. No consequences for sinful conduct; no stepping down so as to reevaluate his or her life in the goal of getting back to a place of humility, wisdom, understanding and restoring intimacy with Christ.

Wisdom doesn't operate in grace without authentic repentance which ushers restoration with God in mind. Pride says, "I can preach God's word of wisdom, do whatever I want and, if I'm caught, my foolish flock will forgive me and allow me to never face my sin." It isn't for me to stand in a critical spirit against this man or his followers, but it *is* for me to function in wisdom and, with that wisdom, righteous judgment within the body of Christ. Wisdom from above allows me and anyone walking in accordance to God's will to judge the body (I Corinthians 5:12). I can do this without wavering in the face of the world telling me I'm being incorrectly judgmental.

According to John 7:24, we see we are not to judge according to appearance, but according to "right judgment", aka the Spirit of God. I have no right in my fleshly nature to stand in judgment of this man. Contrarily, I as a follower of Christ led by His Holy Spirit do have the authority and responsibility to stand in just, righteous, and correct judgment of fellow believers who have gone astray. Admonishment through the wisdom of Heaven will cause me to see only through God's vision as well as aid the wayward person back into righteousness. This goes back to "wisdom from above" as outlined in James 3:17.

Wisdom accompanied with understanding, humility and obedience allow my 'yes' to be 'yes' and my 'no' be 'no.' No apologies, no shame, no guilt. Wisdom from Heaven allows us to be steadfast when Holy Spirit leads. No one can operate is this when pride is abounding. No one who preaches beautifully with great conviction can continue doing so when pride is in effect. They *will* fall. Their sins *will* find them out. Pride overrides wisdom when left unchecked, unrepented, and room to grow. Pride will cause you to attempt to function in wisdom of the Earth which leads away from God and a heavenly mindset. Just as this pastor allowed pride to lead him away from God and into the bed of a woman not his wife, those who allowed him to remain in his position of authority without true repentance or time for refreshment were also basing their decision on a prideful stance. Their pride dictated that they wanted him and so, without consulting the Spirit of God, they kept him right where he was: unchecked, unaccounted sin, and guiding his people in the same spirit of pride.

Pride will whisper and sometimes shout, "You want it, go get it. If you desire it, God wouldn't want you to not have it. Who can judge me but God?" God's people who are aligned with His Spirit are His judges on Earth and we must hold ourselves and others who are called by His name to accountability.

NOTES

CHAPTER 10

HOW LUCIFER FELL

Yet you are a man and not God, although you make your heart like the heart of God—behold, you are wiser than Daniel; there is no secret that is a match for you. By your wisdom and understanding you have acquired riches for yourself and have acquired gold and silver for your treasuries. By your great wisdom, by your trade you have increased your riches and your heart is lifted up because of your riches…you had the seal of perfection, full of wisdom and perfect in beauty. You were in Eden, the garden of God; every precious stone was your covering…by the abundance of your trade you were internally filled with violence, and you sinned; therefore I have cast you as profane from the mountain of God. And I have destroyed you, O covering cherub, from the midst of the stones of fire. Your heart was lifted up because of your beauty; you corrupted your wisdom by reason of your splendor. I cast you to the ground...

Ezekiel 28:2-5, 12-13, 16-17 (NAS)

❧

I have written more extensively concerning this subject in other places so I will, for sake of time, get to the point. Here we see a word being given through Ezekiel to the King of Tyre, but partway down, it shifts to speaking of Lucifer. The belief is that the King of Tyre, a man, was possessed by Satan (or at the very least, a demonic spirit(s) from Satan).

When we realize who Lucifer was to God and all the wisdom God bestowed him, we'll better understand his fall. Lucifer was covered in the finest jewels, perfect in beauty, full of wisdom beyond that of Daniel; that's quite a bit of awesomeness for anyone to handle. Because of the greatness God bestowed, Lucifer became prideful and mistook God's greatness as his own. He wanted to overthrow the King and so he tried; fortunately, his efforts were of no avail. Wisdom is a terrible thing in the hands of the prideful, arrogant and selfish. Lucifer was all about Lucifer, not God.

Solomon's wisdom was far beyond anyone past or present, yet he fell from grace. In I Kings 3 we read where Solomon asked for wisdom just as we are instructed to ask; we must humble ourselves so as to ask and receive from God. He started well but, unfortunately, though the wisdom God granted far exceeded all others, he allowed his self-serving ways and his lust for women to override wisdom. His wisdom never waned; he simply didn't apply it to his own life. This is what happens to countless people from generation to generation.

Job, upon whom I've expounded numerous times, was called "perfect" at the onset of the book. But Job was filled with pride, fear and rebellion and went through everything just shy of death in order for God to perfect him in the end. The only way it worked out to his benefit was to be wise enough so as to use that wisdom to his benefit; he wisely humbled himself as dust and ash. Job is the exception which is why, though he had sin hidden in his heart, once it was revealed through trials and the prophet Elihu, he surrendered. Surrender is the only way to overcome death, the grave, and pride. He stopped fighting the process and relented to God. In this, his wisdom turned into a blessing for himself as well as others.

Since Lucifer fell so dramatically and so publically, he purposes to cause every man, woman, boy and girl to fall in like fashion. God *loves* mankind; hence, Lucifer equally *hates* us. We must be wise enough to recognize his approach and tactics in our individual lives lest we fall away as did he.

NOTES

CHAPTER 11

WISE AS A SERPENT

"...so be shrewd as serpents...(Matthew 10:16b, NAS)."

Definition of Wisdom:

1. the soundness of an action or decision with regard to the application of experience, knowledge, and good judgment
2. the body of knowledge and principles that develops within a specified society or period

Let's begin with part II of this verse. I must admit this is very exciting for me to break down Matthew 10:16 because I've been quoting and praying this Scripture over myself nearly twenty years. However, I've never looked at it as closely as I am now and I believe it profound. What God is instructing in this little verse is vital to Kingdom life and I missed it until recently.

To be guided from such a holy God to be anything like a serpent is baffling, don't you think? Why wouldn't He say, "be wise as Jesus" or "be wise as Holy Spirit" or "God the Father" anything referencing Himself? Upon closer observation, I get it now and it's astonishing to me.

Lucifer is the serpent. He is the one that was the greatest, the wisest second only to God, guarded the Garden of Eden, stood on the high mountain of God; he was the anointed cherub who covers, blameless in all his ways. Nevertheless, he became the least of the least, the scourge of Heaven and Earth due to his raging pride. Once unrighteousness was found in him, because of the abundance of his trade, he was internally filled with violence, and sinned (Ezekiel 28:16). He did not well manage his wisdom to say the very least.

I believe God's intention in this Matthew 10 directive is to recognize this fact: just because someone asks for wisdom, much like Solomon, and receives it, it does not mean they are pure in their motives. Even when they begin well as did Lucifer, Solomon, Job, King David, and others, wisdom can be used for evil. The king of Tyre gained great abundance and wealth due to Lucifer's God-given, God-ordained wisdom.

When in use by an evil one, wisdom will corrupt them and everyone and everything around them. The king of Tyre, I believe, was a man of pride and greed; therefore, he found it adventitious to open the door to

Satan so as to utilize to the fullest extent all the wisdom God had bestowed. He became a human face of Satan in that arena.

We are called to be "wise as a serpent" because it's clear the wisdom with which Lucifer was blessed came from the original all-wise being, God. Yahweh is making the point that we are to be wise as was the worst of the angels because that wisdom proved to be productive for a season; profitable until vileness was discovered in him. It's a proven fact greatness can evolve from the wisdom possessed in the serpent because it originated in purity.

NOTES

INNOCENT AS A DOVE

"…and innocent as doves (Matthew 10:16c, NAS)."

"After being baptized, Jesus came up immediately from the water; and behold, the heavens were opened, and he saw the Spirit of God descending as a dove and lighting on Him (Matthew 3:16, NAS)."

"Because it is written, be ye holy; for I am holy (I Peter 1:16, KJV)."

Definition of Innocent: lack of guile or corruption; purity

Now we'll move on to part III of this verse. Jesus, the Christ, is the eternal dove, but everyone already knows this. We've established Lucifer was filled with the wisdom from God far above all creation. We're instructed to pray and ask for wisdom, if in fact we are desirous of heavenly wisdom. We know He gives wisdom for *all* who ask, and herein lies the "part II" of wisdom.

It's made abundantly clear throughout the Word that wisdom alone is insufficient for spiritual success because wisdom can lead to pride which leads to all destruction. God never intended for wisdom to become corrupted but, as we saw in Ezekiel in reference to Lucifer, it is altogether possible for the perfect wisdom of God through a created being to indeed become violated; hence the third part of Matthew 10:16, "…be innocent as doves." Some Bible versions read "gentle" or "harmless." Equally, these words are synonymous with the term "innocent" and must cease being ignored by those who are called by the holy name of Christ the King.

I've already lent the example of the pastor in Florida and he is one of a multitude of so-called people of God who have an abundance of wisdom, yet they cannot seem to keep their own lives in order. They cannot seem to keep themselves from corrupt and vile sin even while preaching to others. They have not mastered Paul's instruction of "making themselves a slave so that, having preached to others, they will not be disqualified." Their innocence, though they may have begun well, became tainted somewhere along the line of service to the King. Pride of life had to have taken effect in like fashion of Lucifer; they assumed their goodness was their own and not God's who is the only One good.

Never forget how great an asset Lucifer was to God until the fateful day corruption was found in him. And we have no real gauge as to how long Lucifer faithfully served the Trinity prior to his blasphemy; potentially centuries upon centuries, eons upon eons. Never assume that, because one has been faithful to the Kingdom of God a very long time, they are exempt from this happening. We must be vigilant in our pursuit, not only of wisdom and understanding, but of *innocence*, the purity of Christ. Jesus, the "dove", was innocent in every way. There is nothing impure about Him, irrespective of His divine wisdom. To God, *wisdom* and *innocence* are one and the same. It is mankind who, through the delusions of Satan, stains and twists true wisdom.

Again, this is the reason God did not say, "Be wise as Christ, and innocent as Christ." He wrote in metaphor so as to bring everything full circle; to reveal both sides of the coin. It isn't enough to seek wisdom; we must ravenously and with equality be in hot pursuit of innocence, gentleness, and without causing harm to others; God's wisdom always bears good fruit. I know pastors, preachers, teachers, apostles, bishops, and everyday Christians who are obviously blessed with wisdom but they are mean-spirited in their correction and direction. They are harmful to the weak that are in need of wise, innocent counsel. Too many combine their opinions (rarely innocent because they are prejudicial) with God-given wisdom and this is to everyone's detriment.

To refresh, wisdom from above as stated in James 3:17 is first pure, then peaceable, gentle, reasonable, full of mercy and good fruits, unwavering, without hypocrisy. Any other use of wisdom is *not* of God. If I may be so bold as to say, it is from the devil. Wisdom must guide the one possessed with wisdom into holiness as Christ is holy, innocence as Christ is innocent as a dove, gentleness as is the Spirit of God, and so on. Corrupted wisdom is not only useless, it is perilous.

NOTES

CHAPTER 13

A SHEEP AMONG WOLVES

"Behold, I send you out as sheep in the midst of wolves…(Matthew 10:16a, NAS)."

Definition of Behold: to fix the eyes upon; to see with attention; to observe with care

Let us back up to the first part of Matthew 10:16 as it is vital to understand why God instructs as He does in parts two and three. When we read in God's written Word, "Behold," you better sit up and take note! He says He is sending *you*, "you" being anyone called of God, not those with high titles of presumed or self-imposed authority. My book, *Thy Kingdom Come: Kingdom vs. Religion*, more expressly details who you and I are in Christ, who we are in the Kingdom of God; so I defer to it rather than take too much time explaining here. 'You' is anyone who is an ambassador, a son, the Bride of Christ, the Church, or in any capacity called of God.

Too many with titles, e.g. pastor, preacher, prophet, etc., seem to be the ones 'regular Christians' expect to uphold the Word, but the instruction of God is for *all* who accept the high calling of Christ. We are sent out as a sheep in the middle of wolves. We are, in this life, constantly surrounded by those who are evil and purpose to kill us, destroy us, and steel from us. When we are wise devoid of innocence, we will easily and willfully become as the wolves. Many have switched sides without even realizing because they're still referring to themselves as the "wise of God."

"Do not be deceived" is the instruction Yeshua gives to His people. Revelation 12:9 says this, "And the great dragon was thrown down, the serpent of old who is called the devil and Satan, who deceives the whole world; he was thrown down to the Earth, and his angels were thrown down with him." Satan, the wisest of all God's beings, because he is corrupt, is here to use that wisdom to the fullest extent so as to deceive all people. He will not hesitate to manipulate wisdom so as to pull men and women of wisdom into defilement.

It's like the person who is usually wise in Christ. They minister regularly in some capacity to people in need; yet, in their wisdom, they cheat on their taxes because they get nervous about not having enough money to sustain their lifestyle. Satan deceives even those who purpose to be innocent yet allow fear (which is of Satan) to lead them astray. Satan is wise, make no mistake. Christ is wise and innocent which is the more important fact. We are to be conscientious at all times and in all manner of life so that we not allow the wisdom we have obtained from Heaven to become diseased with sin.

The wolves are ever hungry. They're not just in the world, they're in the church disguised as people of God. They have intense wisdom so it's difficult, often times, to discern who is who. The Bible tells us the tares (wicked wolves) grow alongside the wheat (innocent righteous) and they must grow to fruition before we can know which is which. This being so, if we do not purpose just as much to maintain our innocence as we do our wisdom, we will lose sight and become what we hate; worse, we become what God hates.

One of my most favored Scriptures, which was previously quoted, has the words of the Apostle Paul. I Corinthians 9:27 reads, "but I discipline my body and make it my slave, so that, after I have preached to others, I myself will not be disqualified." Old slew foot, Beelzebub, desires above all to disqualify us from the Kingdom of God. He wants to taint whatever God has birthed in us so as to all but destroy your soul. It isn't because he hates us, per se, but because he is jealous most vehemently of God. Jealously is a murdering spirit.

God loves us; in turn, Satan hates us because he hates God. This is why God is a jealous God; His jealousy is the only jealousy permitted among creation. His jealousy is righteous, pure, innocent and holy. He is so in love with us that, knowing Satan's desire of our destruction, He will go to any extreme to protect us from the devil. This is a jealousy that will extinguish the hand of Satan upon our lives.

May we keep our eyes, ears, hearts, minds and spirits upon the Spirit of the Living God and we will not allow ourselves to veer to the right or to the left. Allow the wisdom of God to usher us into the freedom of Christ while living in this corrupt world. Let us maintain our feet keeping them free from the filth of Satan's world system.

NOTES

CHAPTER 14

TESTING SHALL COME

"Some of the wise will stumble, so that they may be refined, purified and made spotless until the time of the end, for it will still come at the appointed time (Daniel 11:35, NIV)."

"Many shall be purified, and made white, and tried; but the wicked shall do wicked: and none of the wicked shall understand; but the wise shall understand (Daniel 12:10, KJV)."

Consider it all joy, my brethren, when you encounter various trials, knowing that the testing of your faith produces endurance. And let endurance have its perfect result, so that you may be perfect and complete, lacking in nothing. But if any of you lacks wisdom, let him ask of God, who gives to all generously and without reproach, and it will be given to him.

James 1:2-5 (NAS)

In closing, the tests of this life are coming, bar none. Note that, in the book of Daniel chapters eleven and twelve, we witness the forewarning that many of understanding (some translations use the word "wise" or "insightful") will fall. They will be "purified, made white and tried" but, on the other hand, the wicked will remain wicked and remain clueless. Only the wise will have any understanding to see past that which they are physically experiencing. Since the book of Daniel is prophetic, we need to be extra cautious so as not to miss the greater meaning.

Before we get into the main verse of this book, Matthew 10:16, I would like to preface it with the knowledge that all the wise will be tested, just as was Lucifer, but many will not pass. Wisdom on its own is insufficient for a successful Kingdom-of-God journey on Earth. Matthew 24:24 points to this fact with the words, "For false Christs and false prophets will arise and will show great signs and wonders, so as to mislead, if possible, even the elect." The instruction of Matthew 10:16 is so vital yet glossed over by most, not excluding for many years myself.

We must realize just how intensely wise was Lucifer and he fell from God's grace. He was God's best of the best, yet he was not sustained by his wisdom. King Solomon was the wisest human on Earth, but he was not successful spiritually. All who are wise in Christ will be tried numerous times throughout this life. Only those who are pure of spirit (aka, those who are led by the Holy One of Israel) will overcome. This is solely because the quintessential Overcomer is their very life breath.

Daniel 12 is specific that the wicked will remain wicked. How many of God's supposed elite, per Matthew 24, will be exposed for the wickedness inside? We must be vigilant in our quest with Christ, sober-minded when we go about our daily lives. It's the little foxes that spoil the vine which translates that we must be wise and innocent in the little matters, not just the large. When we can live James 1, to be joyful when encountering many trials, we are wise because we see through the eye of God; we will see the end from the very beginning.

Let us approach hardship and quietude alike with the same demeanor, the same directive which is to be wise as a serpent and innocent as a dove at all times. I will close this book with Luke 22:31-34 where Jesus said to Peter, "Simon, Simon, Satan has asked to sift all of you as wheat. But I have prayed for you, Simon, that your faith may not fail. And when you have turned back, strengthen your brothers." First we see where Jesus is clear about Satan's intention for mankind: to sift us as wheat. Ouch! How unpleasant that would be. Secondly, Jesus tells Simon He desires for his faith to "not fail." This is very poignant because, shortly thereafter, Peter denies knowing Christ. That is a lack of faith.

These verses continue with, "But he replied, 'Lord, I am ready to go with you to prison and to death.' Jesus answered, 'I tell you, Peter, before the rooster crows today, you will deny three times that you know me.'" Thirdly we witness Peter trying to jump ahead of God. He earnestly wanted to go to "prison and death" with Christ. This is not wisdom, but foolishness simply because the wisdom Jesus had already granted was of little use. Peter didn't want to do as Jesus instructed, but as he desired in prideful flesh. There was no innocence in Peter because his foolhardy pride stood in the way.

Simon Peter didn't merely walk alongside Jesus; he was a right-hand man, one of the anointed twelve apostles. He was an integral part of Jesus' work on Earth. Nevertheless, despite his close proximity to Jesus, pride got in the way. As we all know, he did indeed deny Christ thrice. Innocence was outweighed by fleshly pride. All of us are susceptible so we dare not deign to entertain pride or wisdom absent of innocence.

NOTES

_____

_____

_____

_____

_____

_____

_____

_____

_____

_____

_____

_____

_____

_____

_____

CLOSING PRAYER

Father of all which exists, hallowed be Thy name in all the Earth. I stand in agreement with Your will for my life and the lives You touch through me. Give me wisdom from above that I may speak as the oracles of God with words that are seasoned with salt and full of grace. Allow me the privilege of speaking with the tongue of the learned with a word in season to those who are weary. Keep me from temptation and deliver me from all evil. Open my spirit so that Your Spirit is my only life, and open my ears that I may hear and heed Your voice at all times and in all situations. Pour into me the life of Christ, Your first born Son, that I may become a mature, innocent, wise, understanding son of God. Cause my mind to be unveiled from the deception of this vile world so that I will walk all my days in the innocence of doves while living among wolves. Do not cause my feet to stumble that I may be secure in the Rock of all ages. Purify my heart that Your heart will beat through my body causing me to do only that which Your Spirit directs. Bless You, Oh Lord, for giving me life and an escape from the wickedness of the evil one. Cause me to be gentle so that I will not bring harm with the wisdom you grant. Selah

SCRIPTURES ON WISDOM

"So teach us to number our days, that we may present to You a heart of wisdom (Psalm 90:12, NAS).'

"For the Lord gives wisdom: out of His mouth comes knowledge and understanding (Proverbs 2:6, NAS)."

"The wise of heart will receive commands, But a babbling fool will be ruined (Proverbs 10:8, NAS)."

"When pride comes, then comes dishonor, but with the humble is wisdom (Proverbs 11:2, NAS)."

"He who is slow to anger has great understanding, but he who is quick-tempered exalts folly (Proverbs 14:29, NAS)."

"The one who guards his mouth preserves his life; the one who opens wide his lips comes to ruin (Proverbs 13:3, NAS)."

"The fear of the LORD IS THE INSTRUCTION FOR WISDOM, AND BEFORE HONOR COMES HUMILITY (PROVERBS 15:33, NAS)."

"Even a fool, when he keeps silent, is considered wise; when he closes his lips, he is considered prudent (Proverbs 17:28)."

"A fool does not delight in understanding, but only in revealing his own mind (Proverbs 18:2, NAS)."

"He who gets wisdom loves his own soul; He who keeps understanding will find good (Proverbs 19:8, NAS)."

"Do not say, 'Why is it that the former days were better than these?' For it is not from wisdom that you ask about this (Ecclesiastes 7:10, NAS)."

"This also comes from the LORD OF HOSTS, WHO HAS MADE HIS COUNSEL WONDERFUL AND HIS WISDOM GREAT (ISAIAH 28:29, NAS)."

"DO YOU NOT KNOW? HAVE YOU NOT HEARD? THE EVERLASTING GOD, THE LORD, THE CREATOR OF THE ENDS OF THE EARTH DOES NOT BECOME WEARY OR TIRED. HIS UNDERSTANDING IS INSCRUTABLE (ISAIAH 40:28, NAS)."

"'For My thoughts are not your thoughts, nor are your ways My ways,' declares the LORD (ISAIAH 55:8, NAS)."

"To You, O God of my fathers, I give thanks and praise, for You have given me wisdom and power; even now You have made known to me what we requested of You, for You have made known to us the king's matter (Daniel 2:23, NAS)."

"Therefore everyone who hears these words of Mine and acts on them, may be compared to a wise man who built his house on the rock (Matthew 7:24, NAS)."

"Let no man deceive himself. If any man among you thinks that he is wise in this age, he must become foolish, so that he may become wise (I Corinthians 3:18, NAS)."

"Therefore be careful how you walk, not as unwise men but as wise, making the most of your time, because the days are evil (Ephesians 5:15-16, NAS)."

"Conduct yourselves with wisdom toward outsiders, making the most of the opportunity. 6 Let your speech always be with grace, as though seasoned with salt, so that you will know how you should respond to each person (Colossians 4:5-6, NAS)."

"But if any of you lacks wisdom, let him ask of God, who gives to all generously and without reproach, and it will be given to him (James 1:5, NAS)."

"Who among you is wise and understanding? Let him show by his good behavior his deeds in the gentleness of wisdom (James 3:13, NAS)."

"But the wisdom from above is first pure, then peaceable, gentle, reasonable, full of mercy and good fruits, unwavering, without hypocrisy (James 3:17, NAS)."

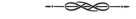

ADDITIONAL PRAYERS

Natural to Supernatural:

Father, in the name of Jesus, I pray that the natural of life become unnatural and that the supernatural of God become altogether natural (**Romans 8:1**). I pray that when I get off track, Your Holy Spirit will quickly correct me and that I will have the grace to humble myself, repent and realign (**Proverbs 12:1**).

Daily Prayer:

I plead the blood of Jesus over my mind, will and emotions; over every imagination, stronghold and every high thing that exalts itself above the name of Jesus in my life and pull it all down into the obedience of Christ (**II Corinthians 10:5**). I command every demonic spirit to be bound, gagged and loosed from its assignment over me (**Luke 8:29**). I release Holy Spirit into my life to be the only Spirit in activity (**Romans 8:14**). I choose today to die to my flesh and my soul

(**Luke 9:23**). Let the mind that is in Christ be also in me (**Philippians 2:5**). I put the full armor of God on myself: the helmet of salvation, the breastplate of righteousness, I buckle the belt of truth around my waist, I take up the shield of faith, allow me to take up the Sword of the Spirit which is the Word of God, and I shod my feet with the boots of peace (**Ephesians 6:10-18**). I choose obedience and humility as I bind from me all forms of rebellion and pride (**I Corinthians 9:27**).

Nightly Prayer or Before Surgery:

I plea the blood of Jesus over my conscience, unconscious, and subconscious mind so that nothing come in on me that is not of You (**II Corinthians 10:5**). I take full authority over my mind (**Romans 13:1**) and place it in Your righteous right hand. I thank You that no dream, vision, spirit or thought come to me from any demonic force, but let that which is from God come to me. Let me remember and understand that You have given me supernatural ability to rightly discern what is revealed and to walk in obedience (**I Thessalonians 5:21-22**). Allow me to grow ever stronger in You and in my identity in You, in the name of Jesus (**II Peter 3:18**).

Breaking Soul Ties:

Briefly, godly soul ties in relation to sexual relations come from marriage **(Ephesians 5:31; Mark 10:7-9)**. Unholy sexual soul ties come from sex outside of marriage be it consensual or through rape (**I Corinthians 6:16**). Both good and bad non-physical (mental, emotional, soulish, spiritual) soul ties can come from strong relationships having nothing to do with sex such as King David and Saul's son, Jonathan, a good soul tie (**I Samuel 18:1**). There was a soul tie between David and Saul which began good and ended poorly (**I Samuel 16:21 & 19:1**) Vows (spoken or unspoken) cause soul ties and also must be broken as vows are a serious matter to God **(Numbers 30:2)**.

In the name of Jesus, I command every evil soul tie between myself and _____ to be broken as far as the east is from the west. Let the blood of Jesus and the Sword of the Spirit sever them forevermore. I ask that You, O God, nourish all good soul ties in my life and break from me all the evil ones, past, present and future. Stir discernment (**I Corinthians 2:13 & 12:10, John 7:24**) from within me to know which relationships are from You and which ones are of the evil one. Stir a willingness and desire to break away from those that are not of You and to nurture those that are. I bind to myself wisdom from above that is pure, peaceable, easily entreated, without hypocrisy or partiality, and full of grace and mercy (**James 3:17**). May I always conduct myself in a manner worthy of the gospel of Christ (**Philippians 1:27**).

Prayer of Peace and Joy:

Father, I come to You in the name of Jesus, the Christ, and thank You for the joy and peace that can come only from Your hand in this very disturbing and chaotic situation (**Philippians 4:7**). Stir up faith within me so that no matter what my natural eyes see, my ears hear, or my mind wants to think, I will receive only that which comes from the Throne of Grace (**Matthew 13:15-17**). Thank You for giving me Holy Spirit to usher peace that passes all understanding, joy that comes only from the Lord (**Romans 15:13**), and discernment of how to handle this according to the Spirit and not according to fleshly emotions (**Galatians 5:16**). May the joy of the Lord be my strength and my utter dependency (**Psalm 28**).

Prayer for Children:

Father, I plead the blood of Jesus over my children, grandchildren and for a thousand generations (**Exodus 20:6**) and thank You that they are the righteous seed of Abraham and are richly blessed (**Galatians 3:29**). I command every demonic spirit of hell to be bound, gagged, and loosed from their assignment over them and I release Holy Spirit to be the only Spirit active as their very life breath (**Matthew 18:18; Job 33:4**). I call forth the warring angels (**II Kings 6:18-19; Daniel 10:11-15; Revelation 12:7-9**) to war against the demonic spirits that are attempting to steal from them, kill and destroy them (**John 10:10**). By the authority and power given to me by Jesus, I cancel every assignment placed upon their lives (**Luke 10:19**) and claim them for the Kingdom of God. I send confusion into the enemy's camp (**II Chronicles 20:22**) that they must flee in seven different directions (**Deuteronomy 28:7**). I thank You in advance that everything my children are going through, it will soon turn for their good and the good of the Kingdom of God (**Genesis 50:20**). No weapon formed against them shall prosper and no words spoken against them shall prevail (**Isaiah 54:17**). I rebuke the devourer (**Malachi 3:11**) and break his teeth (**Psalm 3:7**), in Jesus' name. Father, I give You all praise, honor and glory for the person of God You have called and created them to be, for they are fearfully and wonderfully made (**Psalm 139:14**). I stand in faith (**I Corinthians 16:13**) that nothing will stop them from Your purpose for them. I will not fear the enemy; they are already defeated (**Philippians 1:28**).

Defeated Enemy:

I thank You, exquisite Savior, that You have conquered sin and death and every work of the enemy (**I Corin-**

thians **15:55-57**). I am grateful that You contend with those who contend with Your people (**Isaiah 49:25**). There is no God like You (**I Kings 8:23**) and I and my children are protected from the arm of the enemy (**Isaiah 49:25**). Father, as I stand boldly and confidently before my oppressors, it is a sign of victory for me and a sign of defeat for them (**Philippians 1:28**). You promise that my enemy, though they rise against me, cannot prevail against me because You are building Your Kingdom through me (**Matthew 16:18**). I will not look to the right or to the left (**Proverbs 4:27**), but only at You. You promise to pity the weak and needy and save them from death (**Psalm 72:13**) and that is me.

Bless Those Who Curse Me:

Father, You are worthy to be praised and I give You all praise, honor and glory due Your holy name. I choose this day to allow the hatred of this natural man to be swallowed by the death of Christ and go to the grave to whence He went. In it's place, I choose to put on love, joy, peace, patience, kindness, goodness, faithfulness, gentleness, self-control (**Galatians 5:22**), humility (**Colossians 3:12**), the robe of righteousness (**Isaiah 61:10**), and forgiveness (**Matthew 6:14-16**) that can come only from Christ Himself. I choose to deny myself and put aside all hatred, anger, malice, unforgiveness and things of the like (**Ephesians 4:31**) so that You may be glorified in my body (**I Corinthians 6:20**). I bless my enemy this day and I do not curse him or her. I put on the mind of Christ.

Armor of God:

I choose this day to be strong in the Lord and in the strength of His might. I put on the full armor of God so that I will be able to stand firm against the schemes of the devil. For I recognize that my struggle is not against flesh and blood (even though right now it feels like it), but it is against the rulers, against the powers, against the world forces of this darkness, against the spiritual forces of wickedness in the heavenly places. Therefore I take up the full armor of God, so that I will be able to resist temptation in the evil day, and having done everything, to stand firmly. I have girded my loins with truth, put on the breastplate of righteousness, placed on my feet the gospel of peace. In addition to all that, I take up the shield of faith with which I will be able to extinguish all the flaming arrows of the evil one. I also take the helmet of salvation and place it on my head, and I arise with the sword of the Spirit, which is the word of God. With all prayer and petition, I pray at all times in the Spirit, and with this in view, I will ever be on the alert with all perseverance and petition for all the saints (**Ephesians 6:10-18**).

No Longer an "Old Dirty Sinner":

I cannot thank You enough, Heavenly Father, for allowing me to come out of darkness and into Your holy light (**II Corinthians 4:6**). I thank You that, although in and of myself I have zero worth (**Romans 8:6, 13; Galatians 2:20**), You precious Yeshua, have given me a name with the Name above all names by giving Your Son to make me a son (**John 1:12**). Because of the blood of Your Son making my dead man alive in You (**Galatians 2:20**), I am of a chosen people, a royal priesthood, and a holy nation (**I Peter 2:9**). Remind me of who I am in You so that I no longer allow self and it's emotions to control anything; I refuse to allow self to dictate my condition either way, depression or boasting, as I am nothing in and of myself. Thank You for the honor and privilege of being called by the name of God. I thank You that old things are gone and I have been made new in Christ (**II Corinthians 5:17**).

Life without Lack:

Thank You, thank You, thank You, Yahweh, that there is nothing You have not already provided and will manifest in perfect season (**Philippians 4:19**)! I thank You that, no matter how much I appear to be in debt, I lend and never borrow because the floodgates of Heaven are opened to me (**Deuteronomy 28:12**); I give and expect nothing in return even to my enemies (**Luke 6:35**) because You are the One who brings return (**Romans 2:6**). I thank You that You are revealing to me how to walk in humility and obedience so as to position myself to receive all You have already supplied. I look forward in total faith for the physical manifestation of that which is stored in the heavenlies for me and my household.

Freedom:

Thank You, Almighty God and Redeemer, that You have given me freedom from bondage (**Colossians 1:13-14**). You, majestic Lord of lords, have taken my entire sin nature that afflicts and transferred me into the Kingdom of light and life everlasting (**Isaiah 42:6-7**). I can't give enough gratitude to You that, though men and demons attempt to hold me in darkness due to my sins of the past, You, God of liberty, have given me freedom from my past, freedom from condemnation, freedom from lies, fear, and shame. I repent as dust and ashes (**Job 42:6**) recognizing my worthless estate and receive all Your worth that You so graciously share. I bless You for not only removing the shackles, but shattering them!

From Fear to Love:

You promise that perfect love casts out fear (**I John 4:18**). Father, I don't exactly know how to receive Your love, but I want it. This wicked flesh in which I currently dwell is full of doubt, fear, and unbelief, yet You promise that Your love cast all that aside. Show me, Jesus, how to deny myself and to replace the fleshly nature with the perfect love which only You possess and can give. I submit myself to You as a poured out drink offering and desire to be holy and acceptable to You (**Philippians 2:17**). I choose to allow all that You are to overtake all that I am. I reject fear and anxiety because You care for me (**I Peter 5:7**) and have already defeated my greatest foe (**John 16:33**) and made me more than an overcomer (**Romans 8:37**).

Restoration and Healing:

Gracious Heavenly Father, I thank You that You have promised to restore health unto me, and that You will heal me of all wounds. Many have called me an outcast (**Jeremiah 30:17**) but You call me Your beloved (**Romans 9:25**). You have promised to restore the years that the locust have eaten, the cankerworm, and the caterpillar, and the palmerworm (**Joel 2:25**) and I fully expect that restoration to come about in due season. I trust You, Lord, that it is counted as done though I have yet to see it manifested. I thank You, Yahweh, that You promised that Your disciples (and I am one) have the power to resist going the way of wicked (**Matthew 26:41**), but rather go to the lost sheep preaching saying, 'The kingdom of heaven is at hand' all the while healing the sick, raising the dead, cleansing the lepers, and casting out demons. Freely I have received; freely I will give to others (**Matthew 10:5-8**). I proclaim over myself, my household, my _____ that we are well, healed and whole in the name of Jesus beginning with our inner man (spirit) and then spreading to our outer man (**Mark 5:34; Matthew 9:22; John 5:6**). You bore my iniquities and by Your wounds, I am most surely healed (**I Peter 2:24; Isaiah 53:5**).

Rejection:

When I, the righteous, cry for help, You hear and deliver me out of all my troubles. You, LORD, ARE near to the brokenhearted and save the crushed in spirit and right now, that is me. Many are my afflictions, but You deliver me out of them all. You keep all my bones; not one of them is broken (**Psalm 34:17-20**). For You will not forsake Your people; You will not abandon Your heritage, and I am Your heritage and Your people (**Psalm 94:14**). For I am a people holy to YOU, and You have chosen me to be a people for Your treasured possession, out of all the peoples who are on the face of the earth (**Deuteronomy 14:2**). My people have rejected me, but You, the Almighty, have received me (**Ezekiel 16**). Thank You for loving me unconditionally and without measure (**Romans 5:8**). May I come to know the height, width, length and depth of Your everlasting love and reciprocate it back to You (**Ephesians 3:18**).

Shame and Condemnation:

There is now no condemnation in those who love the Lord, who walk not according to the flesh but according to the Spirit and, since that is the life I choose, I am grateful that I don't have to walk in shame and condemnation any longer (**Romans 8:1-2**). Though my past is tainted immeasurably, my present and future are clean because of Jesus' blood transfusion within me. Since I have been redeemed and Christ is my life, there is no condemnation or shame for me because there is none for Christ.

CATALOG

What was God Thinking? Why Adam had to Die

Looking for God, 3 volumes

Discovering the Person of Holy Spirit, 4 volumes

How to Get it Right: Being Single, Married, Divorced and Everything in Between

Understanding Kingdom Prayer: Praying, Asking, Declaring, Praising

Thy Kingdom Come: Kingdom vs. Religion

Holiness or Heresy: The Modern-Day Church

Navigating the Fiery Black Holes of Life: A Book of Faith

Talking Yourself off the Ledge: Encouragement at a Glance

Walking the Path of Freedom

When All My Strength has Failed

Learning to Digest the Truth

Marriage Beyond Mediocrity

CONTACT INFORMATION

Website: www.thefierysword.com

Email: thefierysword@windstream.net

Phone: 803-238-5166

Made in the USA
Columbia, SC
11 June 2021